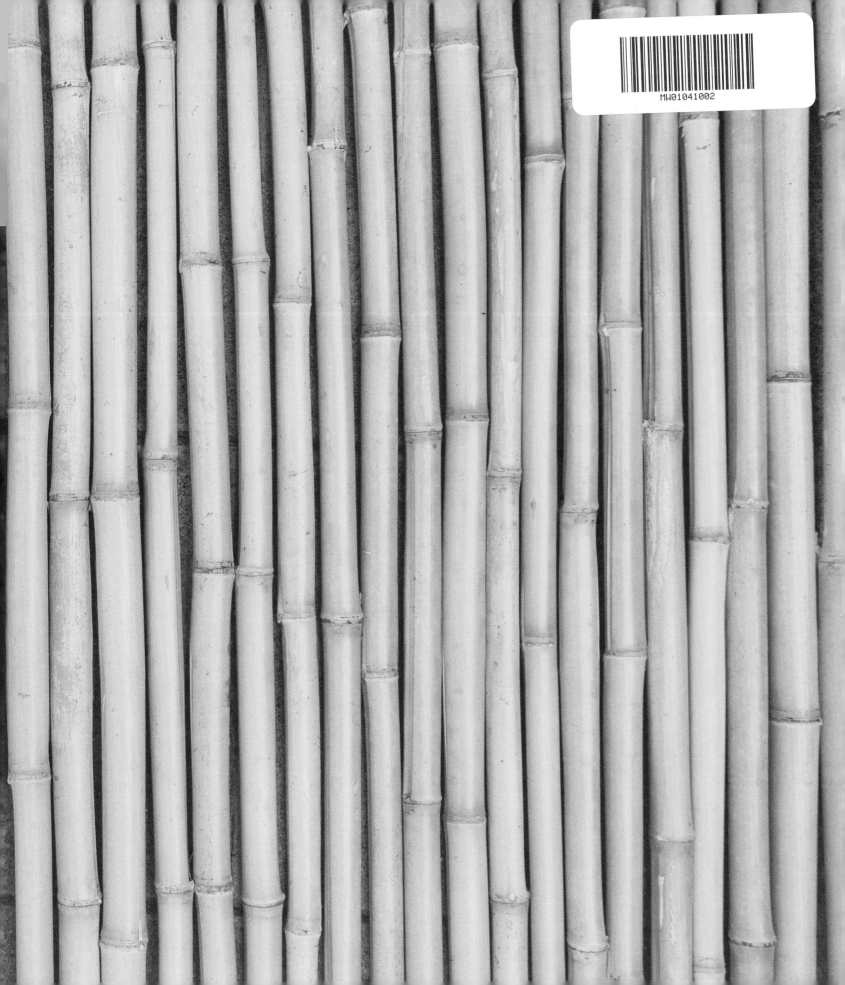

LIVING IN PARADISE

LIVING IN PARADISE

AT HOME IN THE TROPICS BALI, JAVA & THAILAND

ANNIE KELLY

PHOTOGRAPHY BY TIM STREET-PORTER

RIZZOLI
NEW YORK

New York Paris London Milan

THIS BOOK IS DEDICATED TO OUR
LIFETIME FRIENDS
IN BALI WHO HAVE BEEN OUR
GREATEST INSPIRATION, ESPECIALLY
MADE WIJAYA, LINDA GARLAND,
JOHN AND CYNTHIA HARDY,
AND JAYA IBRAHIM.

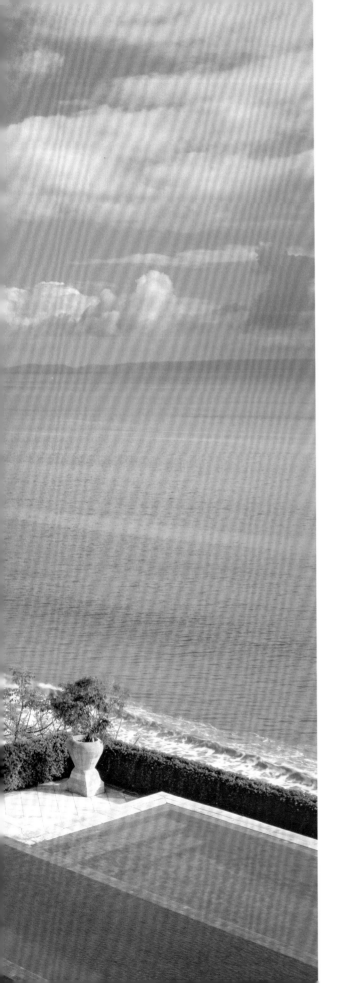

INTRODUCTION

Bali sits like a jewel in the crown of the tropical world, a paradise romanticized in film and song ever since the first Western visitors arrived as tourists in the 1930s. Women in brightly colored sarongs, carrying stacked offerings on their heads, walking in single file toward romantic and ornately carved temples, surrounded by beautiful vistas of palm-tree-studded rice fields, are featured in countless photographs on travel websites today. Even though movies like the classic *Road to Bali*, starring Bob Hope and Bing Crosby, had little to do with the real island, glamour clung to the idea of Bali, and it became a popular destination for travelers in search of exotica.

The decorative styles of Java and Thailand have also had an impact on popular imagination. Yul Brynner's 1956 Oscar-winning film, *The King and I*, introduced the American audience to colorful and ornamental Thai costumes, ceremonies, and festivals. For example, the lantern festival of Loi Krathong and the Chiang Mai Flower Festival are both celebrated with candles and brightly colored woven floral designs, while Thai architecture overall has a refined elegance, which is instantly recognizable, thanks to its ornate and decorative expression. Javanese weddings are also festivals of vivid costume and design. Films and photos show dancers in gilded palaces, or *kratons*, moving majestically in elaborate traditional dress.

When visiting by sea in the 1930s, tourists who first stopped in Bali found themselves in a Dutch colony, with colonial-style houses spread sparingly across the island, integrated with the local mud-walled villages, which were punctuated by stone-carved temples and palaces. Those visitors who stayed on in this lush tropical paradise, mainly musicians, cultural anthropologists, and artists, generally adopted the village style of housing—choosing to live in small houses with thatched roofs and open verandas, all made of local materials.

Who would have guessed that fifty years later these modest dwellings would become the prototypes for some of the most successful resort hotels in the world? Bali is considered to have been the inspiration for this layout, first employed in the iconic Balinese Tandjung Sari Hotel in the 1960s and now the standard design for tropical hotels from the Caribbean to Africa.

The Hindu-Buddhist Balinese devote a great deal of time to temple festivals, and their love of ceremony and color spills over into design, along with intense bursts of seasonal decoration. For much of the year, the temples sit empty of color, until a big festival, when the whole village lines each shrine with elaborate paper, bamboo, and cloth offerings, swags, and drapes. This exuberant decorating is usually for a single occasion, which only lasts a few days, but as a result, Bali has become an island brimming with skilled craftsmen and ornamentalists. Almost anything can be made here—an Ubud roadside sign advertises "Antiques Made to Order," which demonstrates an enthusiastic response to today's design trends.

Much of the tropical style of decorating seen internationally has been heavily influenced by Balinese interiors, especially the contemporary use of bamboo furniture, together with vibrant ikat and batik fabrics. Many New York fabric houses, such as Schumacher and China Seas, have adopted these designs into their fabric lines. Available worldwide, tropical Asian furnishings have inspired international decorators such as Martyn Lawrence Bullard, Juan Montoya, and the legendary Tony Duquette. Balinese suppliers and manufacturers furnish houses all across the tropics, from Mustique to Mexico, Sydney to Singapore. Without huge industrial factories, the local craftsmen fashion furniture,

clothing, and designs by hand that are shipped all over the world. In this way Bali can be considered the epicenter of tropical island design, with influences reaching far beyond this small island, which is only one of thousands in Southeast Asia.

In the past fifteen years, it has become fashionable to import building ideas from Indonesia and Southeast Asia, often along with the craftsmen to realize them. The late singer David Bowie famously used Balinese craftsmen and materials to furnish his home in Mustique, and many designer houses in Hawaii look as if they have been directly shipped from the Balinese resorts of Seminyak and the Bukit Peninsula.

Indigenous architecture in this Asian region is characterized mainly by rooflines. Thatched or covered in ceramic or wood tiles, roofs can reach almost to the ground, sometimes with heavily carved and ornate detailing. Supported by thick wooden columns, walls are not load-bearing, and in the tropical climate of this region, structures are often left open to the elements. Floors consist of simple platforms, raised for eating and sleeping. In Java, these regional houses are called *pendopos*, while in Bali they are referred to as *bales*.

In this book we show many of these design ideas translatable to cooler climates, as most Americans live outdoors in the summer months. *Bales* and *pendopos* can be repurposed as pool pavilions, while draped beds, tropical bamboo furniture, pillow-filled daybeds, outdoor showers, fabrics, and exotic table settings provide great inspiration for both beachside and urban dwellings. Tropical Asian landscaping ideas using creative swimming pool designs and semitropical plantings can be brought into American gardens, since bamboo can be planted in the Hamptons, and the Chinese palm tree *Trachycarpus fortunei* can even survive snow.

The one thing these homeowners in Bali, Java, and Thailand have in common is imagination: unconstrained by conventional ideas and our colder climates, they enjoy happily experimenting with exotic local materials and employing many indigenous architectural styles.

SHARMA SPRINGS

esigner Elora Hardy's architectural portfolio is breathtaking in its originality and use of material. In Bali, Hardy grew up surrounded by rice fields and bamboo, which led to a lifelong love of organic materials. After studying art and design in America, Hardy found herself on top of the New York fashion world as one of the main print designers at Donna Karan Collection and later DKNY. What drew her back to Asia was a desire to make a difference ecologically, taking inspiration from her father, the very successful jewelry designer John Hardy, who has been experimenting with eco-friendly bamboo buildings in Bali since the 1990s.

This elegant and dramatically architectural house was designed and built in about twelve months by Elora's firm, Ibuku Design Studio (a team of Indonesian craftsmen and designers), founded in 2010. Some of the team had only built with bamboo in traditional ways, and the Hardy family's style of curvilinear bamboo architecture was a new experience. For others, their entire bamboo training was learned on the job during earlier projects with Elora's father.

Built for Canadians Sumant and Myriam Sharma and their four daughters, this six-level handmade house rises like a bamboo butterfly with three petal-shaped sets of wings leading off a central tower. Fresh and exuberant, it looks like an organic version of a swooping building by Spanish architect Santiago Calatrava.

This structural core houses twelve huge bamboo posts, each nearly sixty feet tall, extending from a second level stone plinth up to the sixth floor tower roof. The home, almost completely made of a forest's worth of inexpensive bamboo, selectively harvested all over Bali and Java, sits on posts atop large oval stones at the base that resemble overscale organic elephant feet. Hardy is confident of the building's structural strength, as the bamboo is density tested, and even treated against insects with a natural salt solution.

The normal boundaries of architecture disappear as soon as you arrive at the tree-house-style bamboo open tunnel leading into the building, which crosses a small ravine and opens into the fourth floor of the house. Here, the main living space is open to the elements, except for a powder room encased in a giant woven basket. Substantial roof overhangs protect the house, set in a sheltered river valley, from the elements, while bamboo floors radiate from the central circulation tower, which reaches up to the sixth floor, giving way to dramatic views of distant volcanoes above the palm trees. Downstairs flow the bedrooms, library, and spa in organic harmony with the structure of the house.

As it is handmade, this house was built from a scaled-down bamboo model, not from blueprints and drawings. The builders measured it on-site with a ruler and chose a pole from the pile that was the right length and curved at the right angle. This process continued until the model came to life as a finished building.

When Sumant Sharma visited the house in progress for the first time, according to Hardy, he wandered around in silence, occasionally repeating, "I'm speechless; ask my wife, I'm never speechless." Hardy's company designed all the furniture, which she hopes to expand and sell as part of Ibuku Design Studio's range. Long term, she wants to explore craftsmanship using natural materials from around Indonesia and the rest of the world, combining disappearing traditional arts with new innovations. She explains that her former client Donna Karan, who remains an inspiration, calls it "soulful entrepreneurship."

PAGES 10–11: The main elevation of Sharma Springs shows the petal-like structure of the multistory bamboo house.

PREVIOUS SPREAD, PAGE 12: Made entirely of bamboo, the entry corridor to the house is shaped like a tunnel.

BELOW: The main black bamboo supports of the house stretch up to the roof.

RIGHT: A bamboo hammock hangs on a bedroom balcony, with a view over the tropical valley.

Open to the elements, the main living
room has several seating areas.

PREVIOUS SPREAD, LEFT: The basketlike entry leads to the downstairs spa. RIGHT: The tear-shaped entry door to an upstairs bedroom shows the skilled bamboo craftsmanship of the Balinese carpenters.

LEFT: The bamboo dining furniture was designed and made by Ibuku Design Studio.

RIGHT: A close-up of the bamboo dining table features a bowl of local tropical fruits in the center.

FOLLOWING SPREAD, LEFT: The living room sofa cushions are made from handwoven Indonesian textiles. RIGHT: In the garden, next to the spa, sits a hot tub carved out of a single rock.

ABOVE: Tropical fruits, including *jeruk*, mangosteen, and dragonfruit, are
set in a collection of bowls. The silver bowl is from the John Hardy line of home wares.

OPPOSITE: Rattan cushions suround the living space's low bamboo table.
The windows overlook another Ibuku/John Hardy project, called Green Village.

ABOVE: A basketlike structure in the main living space conceals a powder room.

OPPOSITE: An adventurous suspended round bamboo bed is
hung with a white mosquito net and furnished with fabrics from the island of Sumba.

RIGHT: The three teardrop-shaped bedroom doors lead, from left to right, to the outside, a cupboard, and the bathroom.

FOLLOWING SPREAD, LEFT: A basket-shaped structure is used throughout the building for a variety of purposes. Here it hides the refrigerator and some shelving. The bamboo counter stools were designed and made by Ibuku Design Studio. RIGHT: The copper bathtub drain is decorated with a cutout pattern.

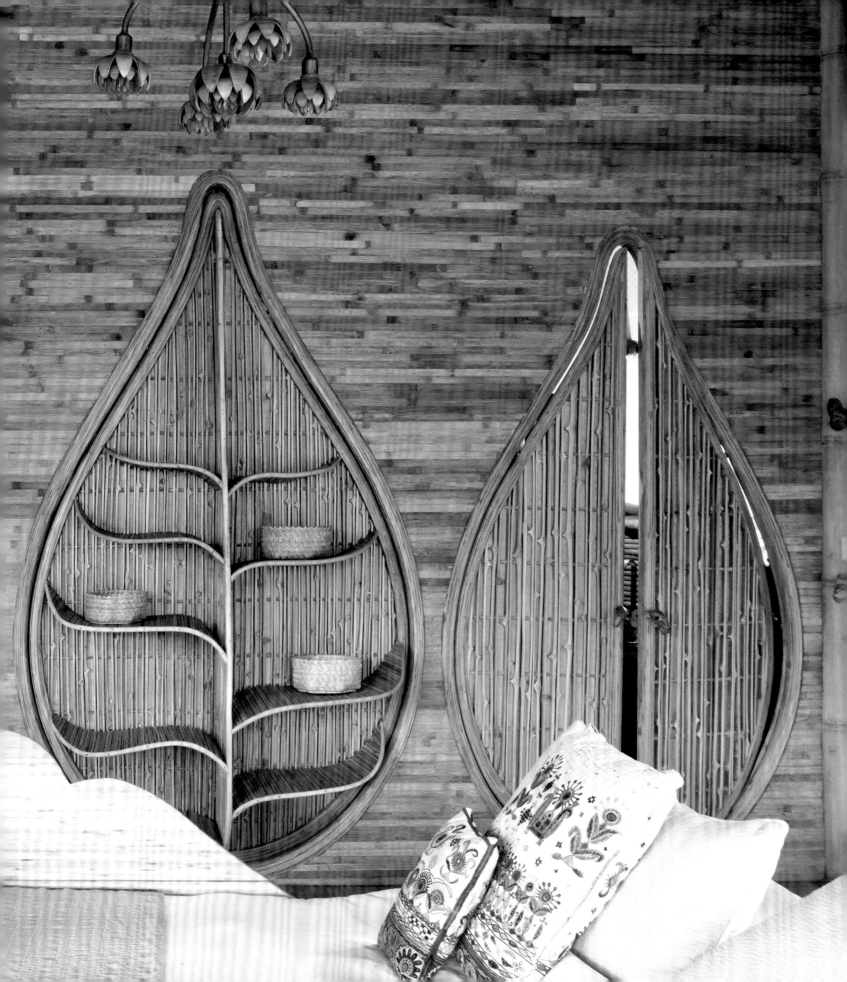

HARTLAND

Hartland, one of the most beautiful rural properties in Bali, lies on the edge of the Ayung River near the village of Sayan in the hills near Ubud. It was built by New Yorker Bud Hart, who started to gradually accumulate parcels of land overlooking the Ayung River Gorge in 2006. Here, he constructed a collection of pavilions and small antique houses centered on a well-placed swimming pool. The property follows the curves of the terraced rice field, which once grew small patches of rice for the village.

Hart has created a spectacular retreat for himself, drawing on the local talents of architect Max Jencquel and landscape designer Ketut Sadru, who worked for the legendary landscape architect Made Wijaya. Hart began by bringing in architect Cheong Yew Kuan to create the original master plan, which now includes an antique Javanese *joglo* as the main house and a smaller building called a *gladak*, which serves as a guesthouse, as well as a more conventional house that incorporates the kitchen. Another pavilion used as a dining room sits atop a series of changing rooms for the pool. These finished buildings have beautifully refined rustic detailing and proportions, complete with thatched roofs and recycled wood floors. Hart brought in up to sixty or seventy workers, who worked daily and shaped the land by hand for over two years.

As one enters through a traditional Balinese gate, the two-acre garden slowly unfolds along a series of landscaped paths. In one direction lies the guesthouse *gladak*, which is reached via a footbridge over a generous koi pond where large orange fish glide in the water. The main living room is outdoors, on the front porch, where Hart added a canvas slipcovered sectional sofa for comfortable seating. This overlooks a spectacular rice field view thanks to an extended wooden deck. With a draped four-poster bed inside and a spacious reclaimed wood bathroom, a houseguest can sleep with the windows open to the cool valley breezes, sheltered under a tentlike white mosquito net. As Hart intended, this is a perfect escape from the rest of the world.

Walking upstream along the edge of the valley is the larger main house, the first new structure, which was built as Hart's permanent home. Here, Jencquel designed a spectacular organic open bathroom below the master bedroom, with a shower that splashes onto a huge river rock and a bathtub carved from Javanese stone. The open living room with its broad deck and comfortable sofas overlooks the fields. Most of the furniture was made on-site from recycled and buried teak from Java.

The long swimming pool, which gracefully follows the contours of the land, is filled with spring water and acts as a striking centerpiece of the property. Most meals are taken next to it or in the open dining pavilion above the changing rooms. Birds flock to the pool's edge, trimming it like a strip of lacework. The rest of the garden can be reached by paths winding throughout the property, where two bamboo meditation pavilions are strategically placed at opposite corners. These are the perfect finishes to this peaceful and contemplative retreat.

PAGES 34–35: The Hartland House in Sayan looks
out to a distant row of volcanoes. Here, a guesthouse terrace has views across
to the main house, which is reached by a wooden bridge.

PREVIOUS SPREAD, PAGE 36: Steps wind up into the hillside garden.

ABOVE: A row of birds fringe the swimming pool.

OPPOSITE: The guesthouse is an imported antique *gladak*
(knockdown wood house) from Java.

OPPOSITE: The infinity-edge swimming pool echoes the curves of the rice field that it replaced.

ABOVE: The master bath shower includes
a large rock as a floor, designed to give the feeling of showering outdoors.

PREVIOUS SPREAD, LEFT: The neat modern kitchen has open roof slats for ventilation and a central island surfaced with wood. RIGHT: A corner of the *joglo* guesthouse pavilion is an ideal place to display Bud Hart's Indonesian textile collection.

RIGHT: The guesthouse living room is outdoors. Sheltered by a veranda roof, the bamboo and cloth blinds protect the furnishings from tropical rainstorms.

BAMBU INDAH

Once through Bambu Indah's bamboo-arched entry, with its floor of large, uneven gray stones, you step into the rich world of jeweler John Hardy, a passionate and romantic ecologist. This small, rustic hotel evolved from Hardy's two main enthusiasms: traditional housing throughout the Indonesian archipelago and sustainable ecological design. Having spent most of his adult life in Indonesia, he created Bambu Indah as part of his commitment to the island, and the project includes research on bamboo as a sustainable building material.

Bambu Indah has a distinctly rustic feel—from the long restaurant pavilion opening directly onto a vegetable garden to the cries of nearby roosters. The restaurant specializes in healthy, organic, low-carb food, which typifies today's slow-food trend, and one of the joys of eating meals here is overlooking the garden from which the food has been harvested shortly before its preparation.

The restaurant is a big part of this dedicated eco-chic resort, which also includes a cluster of antique Javanese houses repurposed as hotel rooms. Here, paths wind through the staked tomato plants and small rice fields to a large Sumatran-style long barn, or *rumah gadang*, built with black bamboo trunks harvested in Java, which sits facing a stone-lined pool.

Among the antique Javanese houses, the building called Afrika is elegant in its simplicity. Set at the edge of the valley, it looks out to terraced rice fields in the distance. In the morning, a row of volcanoes can be glimpsed on the horizon, before a soft cover of cloud veils them for the rest of the day. This two-hundred-year-old house is almost entirely made of hand-carved teak. Large, broad slabs double as front steps, which lead up to the spacious front porch. This is the main living space, furnished with antique benches and chairs. Inside, a strong tribal theme continues, with vintage framed lithographic maps of the African continent hanging above an antique wooden desk and plaited fiber mats covering the hand-hewn plank floor; the same antique wood panels the walls right up to the ceiling beams. Even the bathroom has an open slat wood floor.

Around Bambu Indah's considerable property, which slopes sharply down to the river, Hardy had plenty of space to indulge his innovative ideas—especially in the design of the newer villas. Down on the riverside level, overlooking rushing waters, is a pair of copper-roofed open bamboo structures, accessible via an elevator disguised as a basket that plunges down a vertical tunnel through the cliff. Bathing outdoors in spring-fed pools beside the river is another unique Hardy experience, and he also uses bamboo and copper to create bathroom showers and bathtubs with bucolic views across the tropical jungle.

Easy to miss, a whimsical tree house blends into the coconut palms above the river. With most people looking down to the view, they often fail to see an enclosed bamboo ladder leading up to what looks like a pod for a giant tree spider. Designed by Chiara Hardy, one of Hardy's three daughters, this dwelling sprang from a child's romantic notion of a tree house.

Bambu Indah may not be for everybody—visitors preferring a traditional hotel with tiled bathrooms and immobile floors may find themselves wishing for something more familiar. However, this small hotel is much more in step with the real Balinese experience than the more polished Western accommodations found at the beaches fringing the island.

PAGES 46–47: An outdoor dining platform at Bambu Indah has views over the Ayung River valley.

PREVIOUS SPREAD, PAGE 49: Bamboo pioneer John Hardy re-created a Sumatran
"Minang" longhouse with large black bamboo poles instead of the more traditional wood supports and slats. Here, the structure functions as a meeting space and yoga pavilion for his Bambu Indah Hotel.

ABOVE: A sampling of the homegrown vegetables served in the hotel restaurant.

OPPOSITE: Reworked eighteenth-century Javanese bungalows are part of the hotel accommodations. The hotel swimming pool bisects this corner of the resort.

ABOVE, LEFT: An interior of one of the Javanese bungalows shows its all-wood construction.

RIGHT: A collection of Indonesian textiles, furniture,
and baskets decorates the front porch, which serves as a sitting area.

OPPOSITE: Antique Indonesian furniture is used throughout Bambu Indah.
The practical bed-curtains serve as mosquito nets.

OPPOSITE: A corner of the hotel restaurant displays the food storage and a collection of much-used local pottery.

LEFT: The entrance to the Sumatran-style longhouse is through the hotel rice fields.

OPPOSITE: A casual hotel picnic area is situated by the Ayung River.

ABOVE: Next to the river, Hardy created an organic-shaped swimming pool with a small pavilion nearby.

PREVIOUS SPREAD: The Bambu Indah restaurant is furnished with Hardy-designed bamboo furniture. It serves fresh organic food grown locally.

ABOVE: An open bathroom made almost entirely of bamboo has a view over the river valley below.

OPPOSITE: The bathroom includes a copper sink with a stone countertop.

PAGES 62-63, LEFT: A bamboo ladder leads up to a tree house made from bamboo. RIGHT: Bamboo is also the material of choice for this small pedestrian bridge, which unites the property.

PREVIOUS SPREAD, LEFT: The bamboo ladder ascends to the tree house. RIGHT: Intrepid guests can spend the night in the bamboo tree house with its copper roof.

RIGHT: The tree house interior views the hotel property.

VILLA TIMUR

The late Australian designer Made Wijaya was one of the greatest documentarians of Balinese and Indonesian culture, as well as a renowned tropical landscape architect working in Southeast Asia. Here, near Ubud, he created a country home in a corner of his small hotel, called the Taman Bebek, or "duck field." Although Wijaya was an expert on indigenous Balinese architecture, this neatly ordered house shows he was also referencing his Australian roots—looking at Queensland stilt houses of the nineteenth century as well as the Malay bungalows of the same period, all classic European styles adapted for the tropics.

In the colonial manner, the Villa Timur is built with wraparound verandas, where most of the living takes place cooled by tropical breezes. These surround a tall high-ceilinged room that forms the heart of the house, which is used mainly for sleeping. Wijaya built this house about twenty years ago, influenced by fellow Australian architect Peter Muller, who had just finished the nearby Amandari resort hotel. Muller had removed the traditional Balinese posts in favor of load-bearing walls, a technique Wijaya used to create a central bedroom space. The rest of the house flows around this nucleus. This bedroom features a mosquito-net-draped antique Javanese palace bed, hung with various textiles, including a brightly colored *parang* batik, with a Javanese glass painting of a shadow puppet on the wall above. The tiered thatched roof allows hot air to escape through high-level vents, creating a natural cooling system for the interior.

Next to one of the most famous valley views of Bali, where the Ayung River cuts a picturesque gorge through the scalloped rice fields, the Villa Timur is painted bright, welcoming colors. Set in Wijaya's mature tropical garden, the bungalow (evoking a classic Somerset Maugham tropical outpost) could almost be anywhere in the tropics. However, once inside, the furnishings and interior design are indisputably from this region of Southeast Asia. The color scheme was inspired by a trip to the Banda Islands, although the cutout red entry door designed by Wijaya was taken from a carving he saw in the Caribbean while designing David Bowie's garden in Mustique in the 1990s. The well-worn furniture is from a collection of antique Indonesian pieces seen throughout the surrounding hotel bungalows.

The wide veranda's outdoor dining area includes a comfortable sofa and a set of doors open to a small kitchen. Here, the bench cushions are upholstered with traditional black-and-white checkered cloth, called *poleng*, which is often used in Balinese temples to signify the battle between good and evil.

The dressing room, also tucked under the veranda roof, opens from a large bathroom, which overlooks a small private garden courtyard. This compact house, with its wide plank wood floors and with the option of closing in the verandas to create a versatile sun porch, would function well in any warm region of the world.

PAGES 68-69: One of the many garden courtyards surrounding the Villa Timur was landscaped by owner-designer Made Wijaya. Here is the *dapur*, or Balinese kitchen.

PREVIOUS SPREAD, PAGE 71: The entry to the green-and-red villa includes a Caribbean-inspired cutout door.

ABOVE: Small figurines enliven a colorful Balinese window.

OPPOSITE: In the tropics, many meals are taken outdoors. This is the principal dining area of the Villa Timur, overlooking the valley.

PREVIOUS SPREAD: The breakfast room is screened as protection against mosquitoes. The cushions are upholstered in a traditional Balinese *poleng* fabric.

ABOVE: The bed is hung with mosquito nets and decorated with local arts and crafts, including a colorful sarong in the *parang* batik pattern from Java.

OPPOSITE: Antique Indonesian furniture on the veranda adds to the outdoor living space, which is sheltered by bamboo blinds.

SUMBA HOUSE

Jeweler John Hardy's enthusiasm for building with bamboo in unexpected ways led him to experiment with the Sumba House, which was inspired by the architecture found on one of the thousands of islands that make up the Indonesian archipelago. Unlike more traditional houses on the island of Sumba, this version (built by his daughter's company, Ibuku Design Studio) is almost entirely made of bamboo. The floor is covered in layered woven mats, with a small central patch of adobe floor, which serves as a display kitchen. They added the dramatic, thatched, peaked roof, which is considered to represent the human head; the four main support posts are thought of as "legs" in traditional Sumbanese culture.

On piles, like all ceremonial houses of that region, the building is reached by a series of bamboo steps, via a front platformlike porch. This is where the Sumbanese usually socialize; however, Hardy, in a more practical fashion, has furnished the building's interior with many more conventional seating areas, including a comfortable king-size bed with fresh white sheets. It is rather like sleeping in a house museum, with its walls and doors hung with priceless traditional woven fabrics. Modern touches include seating alcoves set into the sloped walls and a large mirror that reflects the light and brightens the space. The bamboo bathroom is at the back of the house, a location typical in Sumbanese houses, but here we find twin washbasins and a Western-style toilet hidden behind a bamboo half wall. Large, flat slate stones serve as bathroom floor mats.

While moving around the interior and climbing up the bamboo ladder to a mosquito-draped bed high up in the roof, the bamboo building shifts and settles with each step like a living organism. Now a part of Hardy's hotel, Bambu Indah, it can be rented nightly or weekly by the adventurous.

PAGES 78-79: The front porch of Sumba House is constructed entirely from bamboo.

PREVIOUS SPREAD, PAGE 80: A basket of tropical fruit and fruit juices sit on an antique Indonesian stone table in front of the house.

RIGHT: Sumba House's all-bamboo interior shows Hardy's collection of handwoven textiles, principally from the island of Sumba.

OPPOSITE: The master bed is draped with a mosquito net. All of the furniture is made of bamboo.

ABOVE: Skylights add light to the twin-washbasin
bamboo bathroom. Large flat river rocks serve as organic floor mats.

ABOVE: Textiles play an important part of life in Sumba. Woven by women, they carry symbolic meanings.

OPPOSITE: A second bed, or resting platform, displays more of the Hardy
collection of rare Sumbanese textiles. A bamboo ladder leads to another bedroom in the elongated roof.

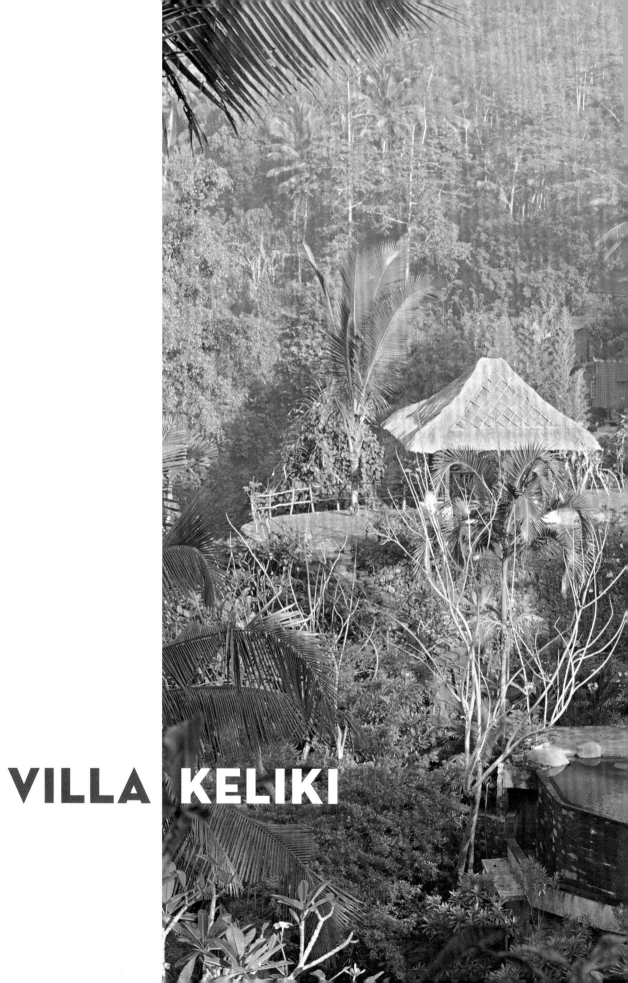

VILLA KELIKI

Up in the hills above Ubud, hidden in a lush green valley, lies a private estate named after the nearby village of Keliki. Through a dramatic entrance gate, decorated with a sculpture in copper by Indonesian artist Pintor Sirait, a series of paths wind down through colorful gardens, streams, and bamboo bridges to various small cottages carefully placed in the landscape, each one representing a different geographic region of Southeast Asia. It is a tour de force inspired by the late landscape designer and architect Made Wijaya's years of working and traveling in tropical Asia.

It is rare to be given carte blanche to develop such a large, two-and-a-half-acre property, but its owner, American inventor and winemaker Bob David, felt the land needed a culturally sensitive and creative designer like Wijaya and wanted him to have a free hand. Australian-born Wijaya was a world-renowned tropical garden designer with projects in locales ranging from Bali, Darwin, Mumbai, and Singapore to Florida. Known for his larger-than-life personality, he was also a recognized expert on Southeast Asian architecture—the author of at least six books on the subject.

Wijaya envisioned a large main house in a traditional Balinese villa style—a big, open thatched roof space for entertaining, with a large master bedroom underneath. Then the small thematic cottages became destinations throughout the landscape, as a way of understanding and enjoying the terrain, which steps down to the rushing river below.

The main house, which sits near the grand entrance stairs, is open to the elements and furnished with pieces collected from all over Indonesia. In one of the four smaller buildings, the Balinese-style house disguises an active gourmet kitchen. Here, in front of an elaborate gilded door, informal café-style seating furnishes the front terrace, which is a convenient location for casual meals such as breakfast.

The rest of the pavilions serve as exotic guesthouses. The carved timber paneling in the Javanese house is from a nineteenth-century antique *joglo* pavilion, with extra panels copied to screen the bathroom from the main room. The bed is a reproduction of an extremely rare eighteenth-century Dutch Colonial–style bed found in a Central Javanese palace from Wijaya's own collection.

Farther down the slope, and over a bamboo bridge, Wijaya designed a Vietnamese-style house. This is a larger structure, on two floors, with a more formal upstairs living space and a substantial Chinese-style bedroom downstairs with decorative paintwork by local artist Dewa Antara. The bed and matching cupboards are nineteenth-century exports made in China, and the table is early twentieth-century Dutch Colonial.

The Malay Cottage is one of the only original structures on the property. Wijaya reworked it using ideas from houses he had seen in Singapore and Indonesia, adding carved panels and bleached fretwork made from teak by his workmen. Above the green antique colonial bed in the bedroom hangs an embroidery panel—a scene from the *Ramayana*, a classic Hindu epic poem—which was found in Banyuwangi in East Java.

The main living space has an enchanting eye-level view of the seasonal rice fields as they progress through planting and harvesting. Called the Singapore Room, this space is furnished in a colonial style, with old Dutch tables, Anglo-Indian chairs, and a large wrought-iron chandelier dropping from the ceiling to add scale.

PAGES 88-89: Villa Keliki consists of a group of thematic pavilions in the hills above Ubud.
Here is the main living bale, or pavilion, with its thatched roof.

PREVIOUS SPREAD, PAGE 91: This Balinese-style loggia provides an informal dining space in front of the
kitchen pavilion. The eighteenth-century-style North Balinese door is a Wijaya reproduction. Late nineteenth-century dining chairs
and a table are positioned below a twentieth-century Dutch chandelier.

OPPOSITE: Stairs lead up though the garden landscaped by P.T. Wijaya, headed by the Australian landscape designer Made Wijaya.

ABOVE: The original house on the property was
refurbished in a traditional Indonesian colonial style with broad verandas and new interior details.

PREVIOUS SPREAD, LEFT: A traditional embroidery panel found in East Java hangs above the colorful Indonesian colonial bed. It portrays a scene from the *Ramayana*. RIGHT: Wijaya whitewashed the living room ceiling and added shuttered French doors that were carved by the Wijaya team and open onto the ever-changing scene of the rice fields above the property. The marble-topped table is late twentieth-century Dutch Colonial, and the armchairs are Anglo-Indian classics made in Trivandrum, India.

RIGHT: Wijaya designed the custom cutout "Sumba Comb" lanterns hanging in the main pavilion, which overlooks the river valley. The nineteenth-century carved Balinese deer is from the collection of Australian artist Donald Friend. The mosaic floor is in a Sulawesi ikat pattern, and the textiles are a mixture of indigo-dyed ikat from Sumba and Toraja, along with a Wijaya "Mud Cloth" screen print.

LEFT: The Vietnamese pavilion was painted red and is situated down the hill from the original house.

FOLLOWING SPREAD, LEFT: A dining corner of the veranda has a view over the property. RIGHT: The living room of the Chinese pavilion is open to the breezes. The locally made chairs are covered with Indonesian fabrics and include a pair designed by Jaya Ibrahim for the lobby of the nearby Four Seasons Resort. The light fixture is a Wijaya design, modeled on East Javanese Chinese house brackets.

PAGES 102-3, LEFT: The colorful leaves in the ceramic pot are cordylines, which are grown in the garden. RIGHT: The bedroom is anchored by an impressive nineteenth-century Chinese bed. Handmade details include a mosaic trim in the floor and the painted frieze around the walls. On the floor is an antique opium mat.

OPPOSITE AND ABOVE: The Javanese pavilion walls are decorated with carved timber paneling from a nineteenth-century antique Javanese *joglo* pavilion, sourced in Bali. The pavilion is on stilts to lift it up for better airflow and views.

FOLLOWING SPREAD, LEFT: The *sketsel* wooden screen is mid-twentieth-century East Javanese. RIGHT: The interior of the Javanese pavilion features a bed reproduced from an extremely rare eighteenth-century Dutch Colonial–style bed found in a Central Javanese palace.

VILLA CAMPUHAN

Here, the passionate decorator and ecologist Linda Garland finally found her perfect client in film director Rob Cohen, as only a filmmaker could appreciate Garland's big design dreams and have the budget to make them possible. Cohen, a keen surfer, was first attracted to the land while he was taking a short break from filming in Australia. He wanted a beach compound for friends and family and met Garland through local environmentalist Emerald Starr. Cohen did not flinch when she proposed a series of Sumatran *rumah gadang* (big houses) around a cooling lake, a plan that also included the importation of Sumatran builders to construct them.

The challenge was to transform traditional architecture with complex ritual meaning into a modern compound without disturbing the ecological balance of Cohen's nearly seven acres of beachfront land. Cohen and Garland agreed that houses on stilts would leave a light footprint and would be open to the cooling sea breezes and also take in mountain and ocean views. The rich cultural layers of the project would give the property a sense of place, especially as Cohen has to fly halfway across the world to reach his tropical dream house. Garland, who founded the Environmental Bamboo Foundation in 1993, was able to take her trailblazing support of bamboo as an ecological solution for the vanishing forests of the world to yet another level of experimentation.

The property is reached through a traditional thatch-roofed Balinese gate, but local references stop there as you turn the corner to discover what at first looks like a Sumatran Minangkabau village. The two largest pavilions are for living and sleeping, and the smaller structures function as guesthouses. With unconventionally high thatched roofs supported by recycled ironwood poles, the interiors presented a decorating challenge. Garland solved this problem by creating separate rooms within using black bamboo screens, connected by antique wood doors. The barnlike ceilings were hung with rare antique carvings from the islands, and the beds screened with yards of tied-back white cotton, giving the bedrooms a dreamy, shiplike quality.

In the open living room pavilion, steps lead up to the back of the space where Garland installed rows and rows of small figural sculptures bought as intact collections from a local anthropologist. Scale was important here, so the rooms are furnished with sizable bamboo sofas upholstered with woven fabrics from nearby Timor, with large ethnic pieces of furniture placed next to them to serve as side and coffee tables. The seating areas are defined by substantial bamboo floor mats.

The master bedroom pavilion has a commanding view of the ocean and is a luxurious combination of draped bed and bathing areas with walls of woven black bamboo. Here, too, the furnishings are overscale, since the high ceilings needed balance. Throughout this space, Garland has added many Indonesian artifacts and carvings—she has lived for over thirty-five years in Indonesia and has become an expert in the tribal antiques of the region.

PAGES 108-9: The Villa Campuhan was built in the style of a
Sumatran village. Here, the owners enjoy a view from the bedroom pavilion through
papaya and palm trees across the ornamental lake to the ocean.

PREVIOUS SPREAD, PAGE 110: A traditional rice storage house,
called a *lumbung*, was reused as one of two guesthouses.

ABOVE: The main bedroom pavilion has a commanding view of the ocean.
These houses are made from recycled wood and were assembled without nails.

OPPOSITE: Twin Brazilian hammocks swing in the main pavilion as if aboard a sailing ship.

ABOVE: Linda Garland used inexpensive cotton, which serves as a mosquito net, to drape a guest bed.

OPPOSITE: The *rumah gadang*, or big house, was built by Sumatran carpenters using
reclaimed ironwood utility poles. Garland decorated the space with a collection of Bali Aga statues and Balinese masks.

Underneath the *rumah gadang*, Garland
added sturdy outdoor dining furniture created
from abstract blocks of stone.

ABOVE: In the master bedroom, ornate and colorful Sumatran cupboards sit in front of a woven black bamboo wall.

OPPOSITE: Garland designed the sofa and added carvings, artifacts, and furniture from all over Indonesia.

FOLLOWING SPREAD: Another view of the main living pavilion shows the large-scale sofas designed by Garland. The shelving displays the owner's collection of small Bali Aga statuettes that were originally assembled by a local French anthropologist.

LEFT: The Balinese statuette collection and other Indonesian figures
are displayed on shelving in the main living pavilion.

ABOVE: The second guesthouse constructed from a recycled
grain pavilion has ocean views.

PURI GANESHA VILLAS

PREVIOUS SPREAD: Puri Ganesha Villas
is a collection of four beach houses
overlooking Pemuteran Bay, on the relatively
unknown north coast of Bali. Each house
has its own swimming pool.

LEFT: A thatched roof beachside pavilion
serves as a cabana.

127

The rich green tropical landscape of Bali's terraced rice fields has caused many an impulsive spur-of-the-moment real estate purchase, and often people return home finding themselves the owners of a piece of land and full of plans to return and build a dream house. Inevitably holiday amnesia settles in, but for some, like noted Cordon Bleu–trained chef Diana von Cranach, it becomes a dream realized. Ten years after buying an isolated strip of beach, she opened the Puri Ganesha Villas in 1997, in the quiet fishing village of Pemuteran on Bali's northwestern coast.

Von Cranach, with her Balinese husband, I Gusti Wisnu Wardana, has created a peaceful haven of four villas and a restaurant, set in a tropical garden overlooking the calm Pemuteran Bay on about four hundred yards of sandy beach. Very few tourists can be found in this little-explored region of Bali as it takes a four-hour drive along winding mountain roads from Ngurah Rai, the bustling international airport in the south, to get there. But the journey is rewarding, as the route includes many traditional temples and beautiful views of the island.

Unlike a conventional hotel, the Puri Ganesha looks more like a collection of private houses. Built in a traditional Balinese *wantilan* resort style, each villa has thatched roofs, high ceilings, and cool tile floors, and is separated from the others by grassy gardens.

Von Cranach has furnished these houses as if they were her own home, incorporating antique doors, carvings, and eclectic fabrics brought back from her travels across Indonesia. Their wide front verandas are filled with antique Indonesian chairs, daybeds, and convenient side tables for gin and tonics.

The two-bedroom Villa Senyum has a dramatic high-ceilinged bedroom upstairs, affording views all over the property. Two-story-tall white curtains add privacy and a formal elegance. Bamboo is very much a part of von Cranach's aesthetic, and she uses it for mats, screens, and additional furniture like small sofas at the foot of each bed. Here, in these villas, she also employs colorful local crafts such as practical small baskets and lamp bases, which add a layer of regional authenticity.

With whitewashed brick walls and carved doors from the island of Lombok, the lower floor includes a large landscaped indoor/outdoor garden bathroom, another bedroom, and a small kitchen. Built before the trend to rent entire villas became an alternative to hotel rooms, this small house was intended to give a family the feeling of owning their own home in Bali, as it comes perfectly equipped and extensively furnished. Each villa includes its own pool and pool pavilion, as well as a beachside *jineng*, or rice loft, with a *klangsah* (woven coconut) roof as a retreat from the hot sun.

The restaurant is defined by carved wood balustrades, reminiscent of nineteenth-century American Carpenter Gothic–style houses, in a design borrowed from the decorative traditions of other Indonesian islands. Here, von Cranach serves truly innovative cuisine based on Southeast Asian recipes, but with a modern twist—often incorporating raw food. She is the author of *Rawfully Good: Living Flavours of Southeast Asia*, and as a food consultant for other luxury resorts, she has pioneered light, healthy menus, so meals at Puri Ganesha become one of the highlights of a stay here on Bali's north coast.

PREVIOUS SPREAD, PAGE 128: Each villa has a slightly different pool. Here, a soapstone-carved figure of Ganesha provides a visual accent.

ABOVE: Unlike the overpopulated tourist beaches to the south, only the local Balinese pass by the hotel.

OPPOSITE: A locally made chair occupies a peaceful spot on the veranda with views across the lawn to the beach.

ABOVE: Each house has been built in the Indonesian style with thatched roofs and open verandas.

OPPOSITE: A private dining pavilion is the ideal location to try out the
cuisine created by owner Diana von Cranach, who is an accomplished professional chef.

ABOVE: Charming vintage Indonesian *becak* furniture is in the dining pavilion.

OPPOSITE: A historic map of Bali designed by famous Mexican illustrator and anthropologist Miguel Covarrubias in the 1930s is on display. His seminal book *Guide to Bali*, written in the same period, is still in print today.

OPPOSITE: The busy kitchen at Puri Ganesha was
designed by von Cranach, a noted cookbook author. She also holds cooking classes here.

ABOVE: Hanging on the hotel keyboard is a
selection of Balinese baskets. An antique carved *Boma*, or demon head, sits on the top.

OPPOSITE: The bedroom doors open to a veranda that faces the sea.

ABOVE: The master bedroom, situated on the second floor of
one of the villas, has a vast thatched roof and offers dramatic views of the ocean.

THE EDLESON HOUSE

After living for over thirty years in Southeast Asia, Americans Mark and Mary Jane Edleson decided to build their own house in Bali. They called upon a Malaysian-trained Singapore-based architect, Cheong Yew Kuan, who many consider the best in the region and whose work is a tropical version of the midcentury modernist architect Richard Neutra. In fact, some of the most influential new buildings in Bali have been designed by Cheong Yew Kuan—the Como Shambhala Estate at Begawan Giri, jeweler John Hardy's legendary "transparent" house at his Bambu Indah Hotel, the Four Seasons Villas in Jimbaran Bay, as well as several other elegant private villas in South Bali.

As president and CEO of the Asia-based Alila Hotel chain (which includes several properties in Bali), Mark has had plenty of experience in how people like to live and entertain. They have always vacationed in Bali, and for a long time owned a small house overlooking the breathtaking Ayung River valley in Sayan, near Ubud. When a neighboring patch of open land became available, the Edlesons realized they had a chance to build something of their own.

Mary Jane knew exactly the kind of house she wanted—an intimate, small house for the two of them, but functional and communicative. The property is entered via a series of courtyards: the first is a parking quadrangle, overlooking a set of inconspicuous garages. Once through the more traditional courtyard gate, a long path leads through the lawn to the house beyond, which has a carefully ordered facade balanced by the landscaping and a glimpse of the river valley beyond through the large glass windows. The two main walls of ornamental brickwork add a strong emphasis to the architecture. The art of working in red brick was at its peak during the fourteenth- and fifteenth-century Majapahit period in Java. Cheong based the brick wall designs on various textiles the couple had collected over the years. These design elements continue inside the house

to become accent walls. Cheong's primarily wooden houses look like part of the traditional landscape of the island as their proportions owe as much to Asian architecture as they do to international Modernism.

The long living room sits parallel to the river, which can be heard rushing below, along with the occasional gleeful screams of enthusiastic river rafters. It is a combination living/dining space, furnished with a comfortable sofa and Indonesian textile pillows.

Mary Jane is an enthusiastic cook, and Cheong built her two kitchens—one out the back in a traditional Balinese style where wood-burning stoves give the local food an authentic flavor and open-bamboo framed windows let in plenty of ventilation. The three-burner oven was designed and built by their son Max, who has an Oregon-based company called Firespeaking, which specializes in natural building and masonary heaters. Next is a modern Western-style kitchen where a long window above the countertop has a view of the lily ponds, which frame the entrance to the house.

To the right of the house are several private rooms—a study that overlooks the lily ponds that in Bali's tropical climate cool the front of the house and a master bedroom with an adjoining bathroom, which would be the envy of any spa. Here, a pair of wooden washbasins has a view of a small private interior courtyard that functions as a bucolic outdoor bathroom with both bathtub and shower. With its large glass windows, the master bedroom takes advantage of the rustic view of the palm-filled valley.

The Edlesons' latest collaboration was with the legendary Australian landscape architect Made Wijaya, who helped Mary Jane, a keen gardener and an advocate of the slow foods movement, to refine the layout of the property. Mary Jane finds that this property on the edge of the river is a whole little cosmos of her own.

PAGES 140–41: The main walkway to the Edleson House was placed at the back of the lot to take advantage of the breathtaking view over the Ayung valley.

PREVIOUS SPREAD, PAGE 143: The house is almost transparent, and the ornamental pond was designed to keep it cool.

OPPOSITE: The main entry opens onto a dining area.

ABOVE: Cheong Yew Kuan's innovative brickwork is based on traditional Balinese entry gates.

ABOVE: The dining table is from the John Hardy/Ibuku Bamboo Design Studio.

OPPOSITE: Mary Jane Edleson is a raw and local food activist who entertains often in this dining space that leads from the efficient kitchen.

FOLLOWING SPREAD: The main living area shows Cheong's intricately designed brickwork and the Edlesons' collection of Indonesian textiles.

LEFT: The ornamental brick wall separates the living area from the kitchen.

CENTER: This modern Western-style kitchen has views of the lily ponds that frame the entrance to the house.

RIGHT: The kitchen serving counter abuts the brick wall. Mary Jane uses local pottery whenever possible.

The traditional Balinese-style kitchen has wood-burning stoves and open bamboo-framed windows. The three-burner oven was designed and built by the Edlesons' son Max, who has an Oregon-based company called Firespeaking, which specializes in natural building and masonry heaters.

RIGHT: The wood-paneled master bedroom features a redbrick wall. The bed cushions are from the Edlesons' Indonesian textile collection.

FOLLOWING SPREAD, LEFT: Cheong, who has designed many hotel and spa bathrooms, created this space using natural materials, including smooth stone basins. RIGHT: This private outdoor courtyard is directly off the bathroom. Here, a spa tub is being filled for a bath.

VILLA KELUSA

A winding tropical road leads up through the hills of Ubud, Bali, to the beautiful and secluded Villa Kelusa, set over seven acres of terraced rice fields, manicured lawns, and lotus-filled ponds. Once through an unmarked entry gate, set into a high wall, and past an orchid-filled gravel courtyard, the four separate thatched pavilions that make up the property are seen spread out across the edge of a ridge, with balcony-like views of a broad palm-tree-filled jungle landscape. Distant blue volcanoes act as a backdrop to this vision of tropical paradise.

Jo McCreary, an American writer and television journalist, always dreamed of retiring to a faraway and exotic island in the sun. So when her son Robert fell in love with Bali during business trips to Asia, he convinced his mother to visit this far-flung corner of Southeast Asia. She loved Bali at first sight, and began the search for a place for both of them, eventually finding it near a tiny rural village called Kelusa.

After they bought the property in 1998, Jo started the building plans, but when the project expanded to include a home for her son, Robert brought in more help, using local Dutch architect Jost van Grieken to add to the property. Recently, they hired fellow American, Lloyd Hassencahl of Design Solutions, a local company based in Bali, to rework the property, and to make it more comfortable. Hassencahl added a layer of his own designed teak and Indonesian mahogany furniture and textiles, and notes that eventually every single surface of the house was refinished.

Once inside the gated property, on the left sits Pondok Surya, one of the two main living pavilions. Windows and an open terrace all have panoramic views with a long swimming pool, which appears like an exclamation point jutting out from deep inside the house toward the magnificent valley below. It is furnished with Indonesian antiques and as Hassencahl explains, "a custom-color wall paint specified by Design Solutions, which was inspired by the adjacent golden rice stalks at the time of harvest." It is also a great place to entertain because it comes with a full bar and small kitchen.

Walking through the well-landscaped garden, reworked by Hassencahl and Jo, where the serpentine river-pebble path flows through the gardens to synchronize with the curved, terraced rice paddies below, is an L-shaped pond that surrounds the central dining pavilion. This building includes a media room—refurnished by Hassencahl, who added the upholstery—turned-wood side table lamps inspired by Hindu ceremonial candleholders, and a large kitchen. This long thatched-roof building looks like a contemporary version of a barn.

Nearby, the two-story sleeping pavilion was built with tall glass windows designed to look transparent when the curtains are drawn back, in order to reveal the magnificent view. Here, two large comfortable bedrooms have been placed at the front of the building, and the bathrooms and a small ground floor study completes the rear.

The northern most pavilion is designed as a pool house. Hanging chairs, chaises, wicker chairs, and Indonesian details provide plenty of space to relax and read a book. At the far end of the garden sits a sculpture garden, designed by Jo and Lloyd as a combined project, with each piece carefully placed in harmony with one another. This sense of balance and proportion is echoed throughout the property.

PAGES 158–59: At Villa Kelusa, the dining pavilion, called the Pondok Sapi, overlooks one of two swimming pools and the Pakuseba River valley beyond.

PREVIOUS SPREAD, PAGE 161: Stretching out into the landscape, the infinity pool is accessed from the Pondok Surya, one of four living pavilions.

OPPOSITE: The eight-acre garden was landscaped by owner Jo McCreary and designer Lloyd Hassencahl.

ABOVE: Indonesian wooden craft objects, collected for their shape and texture, fill a niche in one of the living pavilions. The swimming pool spills out from this indoor space.

ABOVE: Hassencahl added woven cane chairs to the dining pavilion.

OPPOSITE: A very early Indonesian stone carving fills the niche next to the bathroom.
A landscaped interior courtyard can be seen through the door.

FOLLOWING SPREAD, LEFT: Local textiles enliven a bench in the media room.
RIGHT: A dressing table in one of the upstairs bedrooms is tucked into an alcove.

LEFT: The Pondok Sapi is one of the principal living spaces of the Villa Kelusa. Here, meals are served from the Indonesian-style kitchen.

ABOVE: A detail of the hand-carved wooden pails is shown next to the ornamental pool.

CEGER

Jakarta, where the sound of the *adzan* (call to prayer) echoes poetically over its smoggy rooftops, is a long way from the capital cities of Europe. This huge sprawling Indonesian city, which is the political and financial center of the country, was the home of the late well-known international decorator Jaya Ibrahim, who was very much a product of its cultural mix.

He began his career as a designer in the 1970s, working in England for the New Zealand–born decorator Anoushka Hempel, best known for her Asian-inspired London hotel, Blakes.

With his sophisticated and studied sensibility, Ibrahim was able to incorporate his influences from abroad and his deep understanding of traditional Indonesian design in much of his work, which now includes hotels and homes from Mexico to Paris and all across Asia. He founded Jaya International Design, his decorating and architectural business, over twenty years ago. The company then branched out to include business partner Bruce Goldstein and extended to offices in Singapore, Shanghai, and New York.

At home, hidden away from the chaotic and noisy street, a courtyard gate opens to a small landscaped courtyard, which forms a barrier to the world outside. Tall doors open to reveal an entrance staircase leading to the lower floors, which served as Ibrahim's office, and to the upper floor, where he added a living space that Ibrahim shared with his associate, John Saunders, as well as a large conference room and library.

Lined with a collection of antique Indonesian terra-cotta pots, the entry landing is a calm ordered space. From here, doors open to a long living room, which includes a dining table for informal meals and a small workspace overlooking a tree-filled park at the rear of the property. The sitting area is defined by tall movable screens of clear glass that are hung with a series of decorative prints. These continue around the room, helping to unite the space, although Ibrahim also added texture and depth to the walls by hanging carved screens and ornate finials above the doors. To divide the space, Ibrahim displayed a collection of fourteenth-century Javanese and Thai bowls on stacks of lacquered Chinese trunks, made more eye-catching by placing them on plinths cut from short lengths of wood.

Like the late American decorator Tony Duquette, Ibrahim added the unexpected to his walls to give them more structure and definition. Above his bed you will see a gilded mirror on a fabric panel hung on the wall, which becomes a graphic background to a selection of framed prints and his collection of small boxes at the head of the bed. Gold striped walls act as a backdrop around the room to a series of architectural prints in gold frames. Built-in lacquered white side tables running around the room add a crisp modern look and a sense of greater order to the space.

The master bathroom leads from the bedroom and is as richly decorated as the rest of the house. A small chaise overlooks the tree-filled view at the back of the house, and the more functional wash spaces are tucked away in private alcoves.

On weekends, the design duo headed for the beautiful and much published Cipicong, Ibrahim's large country house, which overlooks a volcano. "My first impulse," explained Ibrahim, shortly before his tragic and accidental death last year, "is to seek beauty and serenity, rather than adhere to one period."

PAGES 170-71: The main sitting room in Ibrahim's Jakarta town house, Ceger, overlooks the entry courtyard.

PREVIOUS SPREAD, PAGE 172: Ibrahim's workspace includes a desk of his own design, as well as his research library.

LEFT: The master bedroom contains part of Ibrahim's collection of Southeast Asian lacquerware. Under the side tables are a collection of dim sum boxes. Above the bed hangs a Javanese-European-style mirror.

OPPOSITE: Ibrahim collected rare Majapahit terra-cotta
temple towers, which he displayed on tall pedestals. Here, one is framed by a doorway.

ABOVE: Every surface of the apartment is filled with a carefully
considered display of colors and shapes. Even the red lampshades are part of the composition.

FOLLOWING SPREAD, LEFT: A daybed is positioned in the master bathroom to provide
a view of the garden. RIGHT: An eclectic mix fills a corner of the entrance.
A stripped English hall chair is paired with Chinese trunks, a Majapahit pot, and a pedestal
bearing the Ibrahim company logo.

OPPOSITE: A conference table occupies half of the living room. The furniture and lighting
are from the Ibrahim line of furniture. The plates on the wall are Kitchen Ming.

ABOVE: A dining table is set with Chinese plates. The candlesticks are from the Ibrahim line of accessories.

CIPICONG

Although decorator Jaya Ibrahim's country house, Cipicong, has been the focus of many books and magazines and has inspired decorators worldwide, it is worth another look. This romantic retreat is the Asian version of a Palladian villa where Ibrahim gave the house exquisite proportions, carefully balancing the design elements of each facade. He built this property as a retreat for himself and his partner, John Saunders, and in doing so created a comfortably cool, well-ventilated house that could function well anywhere in the world.

Ibrahim distilled the best of his ideas here, designing much of the furniture himself with the help of excellent local craftsmen. He was influenced by many cultural sources and chose to layer Dutch Colonial design with elements of the rich Javanese culture of his childhood. Ibrahim had a keen sense of proportion and balance, which you can see in the formal arrangements of his possessions.

Visitors arrive along a rustic drive and ascend a series of formal steps to the north-facing main entrance of the house. The first main space is a majestic dining room, which opens onto a deeply exotic interior courtyard, with glass lanterns hung along the surrounding open passageways. This courtyard is lit at night by the orange glow of ceramic pots on the ground, making it a magical place.

Throughout the one-story house, Ibrahim built the ceilings high—the traditional way to keep rooms cool in hot climates. A series of smaller rooms open off the central dining room, creating private spaces for friends and family. Breakfast and lunch are served in a covered loggia along the south facade, screened from the morning sun by bamboo blinds.

On the other side of the house is a large library, where Gothic-style windows give a view of the countryside and the reflecting pool. Here Ibrahim's collections of books, fabrics, Asian ceramics, and Dutch artifacts—acquired over a lifetime of traveling—are displayed, all carefully arranged in perfect compositions based on shape and texture. The nearby master bedroom has his trademark layer of fabrics and textures on the walls, with a screen behind the bed instead of a conventional headboard, and a central mirror hung on an antique cloth. It all combines to create a room of deep exoticism, which is typical of Ibrahim's own personal taste.

PAGES 182–83: Ibrahim placed a row of Indonesian waterpots to define the edge of an ornamental pond at Cipicong. The eroded Javanese volcano Gunung Salak can be seen in the distance.

PREVIOUS SPREAD, PAGE 185: The house is a broad sequence of rooms surrounding two inner courtyards. Here, in the main living courtyard, small ceramic pots contain candles, which are lit at night.

RIGHT: The main reception area of the house, or *pendopo*, is reached by a broad staircase. In front is a large formal garden planted with coconut trees in a grid.

OPPOSITE: Another view of the principal central courtyard shows it
surrounded by a veranda on all sides and centered by a Majapahit-era pot within the fountain,
which dates back to the fourteenth century.

ABOVE: Ibrahim filled the table in a courtyard seating area with his
collection of antique Indonesian pottery. The cushions are made from Javanese batik fabric.

PREVIOUS SPREAD, LEFT: Ibrahim was a master of the cultural mix.
Here, on top of a Dutch Colonial cupboard he assembled a collection of jade-colored
Chinese pottery, eighteenth-century European prints, mirrors topped
with Javanese gold headdresses, and a vintage Indonesian metal tray. RIGHT: In a corner
of the master bedroom, Ibrahim topped a Javanese *kemben*
batik with gilded antique wooden finials.

ABOVE: An assemblage of green jade-colored pottery sits on a side table.

OPPOSITE: A corner of the library shows Ibrahim's
collection of green Dutch Colonial plates and framed antique Indonesian prints.

34. Djokjakarta. Een der poorten van den Kraton.

OPPOSITE: Furnished with antique-style Indonesian furniture, the breakfast loggia
outside the kitchen is at the rear of the house.

ABOVE: A dreamy collection of antique European glass decanters
tipped with gold sits in front of a bedroom mirror.

ABOVE, LEFT: In a guest bedroom Ibrahim assembled a collection of
Asian furnishings and china displayed as tablescapes. The fabrics are all Indonesian.

ABOVE, RIGHT: A small Javanese hand-colored print hangs on a red wall.

OPPOSITE: The master bedroom shows Ibrahim's genius at room arranging.
He used almost entirely Indonesian furniture and furnishings in a tropical colonial style.

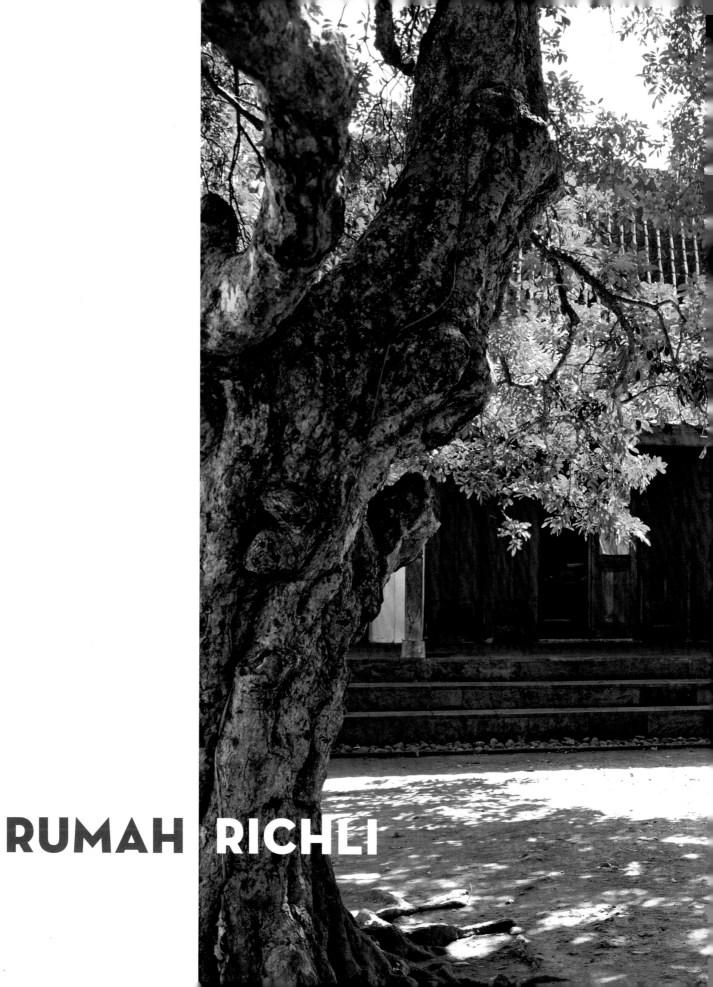

RUMAH RICHLI

When François Richli and his then-wife, Olivia, were chosen by hotelier Adrian Zecha to open the latest jewel in his crown of Aman hotels, the Amanjiwo (designed by Ed Tuttle in 1997), they decided to lease a house in a nearby village. With two small children, they needed a place of their own, away from the incessant activity of the hotel, especially since both parents worked there—François as the general manager, and Olivia seemingly in charge of everything else.

They found a traditional Javanese wooden house in the village of Pangonan not far from the magnificent Buddhist monument of Borobudur, which was the inspiration for Tuttle's groundbreaking design of the Amanjiwo. This simple and rustic property is quite a contrast to the formal stateliness of the nearby hotel—it is simply a series of rooms surrounding a central courtyard.

The main entry is through a large pair of wooden gates, where a veranda runs around the courtyard, providing more living space in the sometimes cooler outdoors in the tropical evenings. The house had been used by the village as a meeting place, so the sitting room was large with plenty of windows, which attracted the Richlis. Here, they placed the furniture they had collected on their travels across Indonesia between the four main supporting columns on a central natural fiber floor mat, which defined the space. They also added reclaimed doors from the island of Madura, leading through to the dining room, where the sociable couple did plenty of entertaining. They installed glass roofing tile to bring in more light and opened up some of the rooms for a better flow.

White stucco walls and a new polished concrete floor, along with plain and comfortable furnishings, form a backdrop to the couple's striking collections of Indonesian artifacts. Suspended poles around the living room became a great solution to display Olivia's collection of traditionally woven ikat and sonkat fabrics. The ceilings were quite high once they had been opened up—adding a sense of grace and proportion—and the natural wood texture of the rafters works well with the Indonesian chairs and tables. Although quintessentially Javanese, this is a room that could be duplicated anywhere in the world.

Today, the children have grown up, and Olivia manages the Heckfield Place hotel in Hampshire. François himself recently reclaimed the house after managing many other hotels around the world—the siren song of exotic Java called him back to the simple village he calls home.

PAGES 198–99: The entry courtyard of the Rumah Richli house in Pangonan, Java, features a venerable *kelengkeng* tree.

PREVIOUS SPREAD, PAGE 200: The main living area features many natural materials and textures. Clear glass block skylights bring light into the space. This was once the village meeting room.

ABOVE: A bamboo daybed sits at one end of the room. The floor is poured concrete that was redone by François Richli.

OPPOSITE: A pair of antique Indonesian sofas flanks an Indonesian colonial table.

PREVIOUS SPREAD, LEFT: Viewed from the courtyard,
the library occupies an open loggia. RIGHT: A traditional Javanese bathroom has
been updated with hot water and Western fixtures.

ABOVE: A pair of Javanese trance horses hangs above an antique chest.

OPPOSITE: The sunny kitchen includes traditional Indonesian
furniture and a rustic organic teak dining table.

ABOVE: A collection of handmade vases sits on a kitchen shelf.

OPPOSITE: An antique bed centers the master bedroom. The ceiling is made of *bedeg*, or woven bamboo.

ED TUTTLE

Although American architect Ed Tuttle now lives in Paris, he has had a lifelong love affair with Southeast Asia. Back in the late 1960s and early 1970s, Tuttle spent a formative seven years in this culturally vibrant part of the world, and now he specializes in hotel design in Thailand and Indonesia, as in well as in many resort areas across Asia. Tuttle started his firm Design Realization in Paris back in 1977, and since then he has been responsible for some of the most elegant boutique hotels in the world. As with his pioneering design for the Amanpuri in Phuket, Thailand, Tuttle likes to base his work on some aspect of local indigenous architecture and works through each aspect of interior design in order to achieve a harmonious whole.

Frequently the architect of choice for the elegant Aman resorts, Tuttle designed a retreat for himself next to the Amanpuri. The first Aman hotel, it opened in 1988 and quickly attracted attention as a new concept in boutique hotels, not just for Tuttle's sympathetic re-creation of traditional Thai architecture but also for the hotel's absence of a front desk, a minibar, or a lobby. Now absorbed into the Amanpuri, Tuttle's villa can be rented for the night but still retains the elegant architectural detailing that can be widely seen across the resort, even though his personal collection of art and scupture is no longer in place.

When hotelier Adrian Zecha first bought the land and signed with Tuttle to design a resort, they both quickly realized that its greatest asset was the cliffside ocean views and that the best way to take advantage of this was to go small. Rather than building a big hotel-like edifice, Tuttle envisioned a series of small stepped down pavilions, designed in a traditional Thai style with swooping ornamented roofs and modern architectural twists. This includes his own villa, which sits parallel to the ocean and was planned to house his growing collection.

For structural reasons, Tuttle used concrete for both the pavilion platforms and their supporting columns, which he then sheathed in wood veneer. This also prevented undermining by termites, a problem common in the tropics.

In the villa's entry courtyard, Tuttle brought in a traditional Thai door, painted and hung as a piece of outdoor sculpture. The first room is furnished somewhat in the traditional Thai style, with a big flat daybed, doubling as a sofa, with traditional triangular Thai cushions that act as backrests.

Tuttle used open screen paneling throughout the Amanpuri, backing the panels with mirror for his bathroom or with wood to form low interior walls. He also created glass-shelved niches for his collection of Thai statuary and decorative objects; the larger pieces were given their own stands. Two large pavilions sit at each end of the swimming pool, one for dining and the other for living—both easily customized for entertaining large groups of friends.

PAGES 210–11: Ed Tuttle's property has a fine view of the ocean in Phuket, Thailand.

PREVIOUS SPREAD, PAGE 213: A pavilion based on traditional Thai architecture anchors one end of the pool.

ABOVE: A gilded coffee table holds a collection of Southeast Asian antiques.

OPPOSITE: A large antique wooden Buddhist figure presides
over one end of a pavilion. The low table in the foreground is set for a meal.

ABOVE: A reclaimed temple gate makes a backdrop for a contemplative Buddha.

OPPOSITE: Another Thai-style pavilion sits at the other end of the pool. This functions as a living space.

FOLLOWING SPREAD, LEFT: An outdoor courtyard can be entered from the bathroom.

RIGHT: The spa bathroom is decorated with Southeast Asian antiques. It features an enclosed wooden tub.

The ridge line of Bambu Indah's resturant's roof is enlivened by a cast of traditional Indonesian figures.

RESOURCES

HOTELS & VILLAS TO RENT

Amanpuri
Phuket Island, Thailand
www.aman.com/resorts/amanpuri

Bambu Indah
Sayan, Ubud, Bali, Indonesia
www.bambuindah.com

Cinta Inn
(Cinta Grill)
Ubud, Bali, Indonesia
www.cintainn.com

Green Village Bali Houses to Rent
Abiansemal, Bali, Indonesia
www.greenvillagebali.com

Hartland Estate
Sayan Ridge, Ubud, Bali, Indonesia
www.hartlandestate.com

Puri Ganesha Villas by the Sea
Pemuteran, Gerokgak, Singaraja,
Bali, Indonesia
www.puriganesha.com

Sharma Springs
Abiansemal, Bali, Indonesia
www.greenvillagebali.com/houses
/sharma-springs

Taman Bebek Bali
Sayan Ridge, Ubud,
Bali, Indonesia
www.tamanbebekbali.com

Villa Campuhan
Karangasem, Bali, Indonesia
www.villacampuhan.com

Villa Keliki
Tegalalang, Bali, Indonesia
www.villakeliki.com

Villa Kelusa
Kelusa, Bali, Indonesia
www.villakelusa.com

ARCHITECTS & DESIGNERS

Arief Rabek
Indobamboo
Klungkung, Bali, Indonesia
www.indobamboo.com

Cheong Yew Kuan
AreaDesigns
Singapore
info@areadesigns.com

Ed Tuttle
Design Realization
Paris, France
designrealization@designrealization.net

Elora Hardy
Ibuku Design Studio
Sayan, Ubud, Bali, Indonesia
www.ibuku.com

I Nyoman Miyoga
P.T. Ramawijaya International Design
Denpasar, Bali, Indonesia
www.ptramawijaya.com

Lloyd Hassencahl
Design Solutions
Ubud, Bali, Indonesia
www.designsolutionspt.com

Mark Keatingue
P.T. Bale Gede Internasional
Sanur, Bali, Indonesia
www.tropicalbuildings.com

SHOPPING IN INDONESIA

Biasa
Clothing and Accessories
Jalan Danau Tamblingan 37, Sanur, Bali,
Indonesia; Jalan Raya Batu Belig 9, Kerobokan,
Bali, Indonesia; Jalan Raya Sanggingan, Ubud,
Bali, Indonesia; Jalan Raya Seminyak 36, Kuta,
Bali, Indonesia
www.biasagroup.com

Cannan Boutique & Gallery
Katamama Hotel
Jalan Petitengent 51B
Seminyak, Bali, Indonesia
www.canaanbali.com

Gaya Ceramic
Jalan Raya Sayan 105, Ubud, Bali, Indonesia
www.gayaceramic.com

Jean-François Fichot
Jewelry and Home Decor
Jalan Pengosekan
Ubud, Bali, Indonesia
www.jf-f.com

John Hardy Ubud Workshop and Showroom
Abiansemal, Bali
www.johnhardy.com

Kevala Ceramics and Kevala Home
Denpasar, Bali, Indonesia
www.kevalaceramics.com

Rio Helmi Gallery
Jalan Suweta 24A, Ubud, Bali, Indonesia
www.riohelmi.com

Threads of Life
Jalan Kajeng 24, Ubud, Bali, Indonesia
www.threadsoflife.com

Unearth Space
South Jakarta, Jakarta, Indonesia
www.canaanbali.com

SHOPPING IN THE USA

1stDibs
www.1stdibs.com

Anthropologie
www.anthropologie.com

Berbere World Imports
Inglewood, California
www.berbereworldimports.com

Cost Plus World Market
www.worldmarket.com

Jalan Jalan Imports
Topanga, California
www.jalanjalanimports.com

Kembali Collective
Long Beach, California
www.kembalihome.com

MISCELLANEOUS

Green School
www.greenschool.org
Founded by John and Cynthia Hardy, Green
School has an inspiring approach to education.
The school, begun in the rice fields of Bali
in 2008, consists of a tailor-made campus of
innovative bamboo structures that has
grown to accommodate four hundred students.
Tours are available.

Linda Garland designed this bridge as a room across the river at
Panchoran, her estate in Nuh Kuning, Bali.

ACKNOWLEDGMENTS

We would like to thank the Balinese people for their incredible hospitality over the years, especially the staff at Made Wijaya's Taman Bebek resort in Sayan. Thanks also to the friends who let us document their homes, as well as the houses and hotel projects they designed for their clients.

We have been dazzled by the many rich cultures of Indonesia since the late 1970s when we were lucky enough to meet some of the *Living in Paradise*–profiled designers, who were just starting out in their careers. Back then environmentalist and designer Linda Garland had opened a chic beachside store, selling textiles. A few years later her then-husband, entrepreneur Amir Rabik, encouraged by Mick Jagger and Jerry Hall's wedding held in one of his early structures, started to design buildings using local materials, including bamboo and thatched roofing. At the same time, landscape designer and architect Made Wijaya was attempting to maintain and preserve the Balinese tradition of building with mud brick, which today has sadly been supplanted by more durable concrete block. He used mud brick for a local family's compound and was beginning to design gardens. Meanwhile, Balinese designer Putu Suarsa was starting to build with bamboo, a trend that fully expresses itself today with the freeform Calatrava -like structures of Ibuku Design Studio. Also, during this period jet-set Indonesian photographer Rio Helmi was documenting the rich tribal traditions of the thousands of islands in the Indonesian archipelago.

Later on, we were fortunate to be introduced to Indonesia's most influential decorator, Jaya Ibrahim, and his partner, John Saunders, on a trip with Made Wijaya to the island of Sumatra, where Ibrahim's grandfather had founded a Muslim school for girls. Some of our finest memories of Java come from staying in Cipicong, Ibrahim's beautiful villa in the rice fields.

During one of our many trips to the region we met Indonesian artist and sculptor Pintor Sirait, a frequent collaborator of Made Wijaya's, and bon vivant musical scholar Asri Gaftar, whose property overlooking the beach in Bali is so elegantly pared down that it was near impossible to convey the dramatic setting in photographs.

Thank you to Singapore architect Cheong Yew Kuan, the "tropical Richard Neutra," for giving us permission to include the Edleson House in Sayan.

Thanks also to artist Karim Rabik and his brother Arief, founder of Indobamboo, who is carrying his mother Linda Garland's pioneering work with bamboo to the next step. And to Elora Hardy, whose firm Ibuku Design Studio is also a family legacy. Elora has taken her father John Hardy's passion for sustainable design into the future.

We were inspired by Lombok-based American author Jamie James's description of expats in Asia in his recent book *The Glamour of Strangeness: Artists and the Last Age of the Exotic*. Designer Lloyd Hassencahl and Bud Hart helped us considerably, while Diana von Cranach's cuisine and hospitality at the Puri Ganesha Villas were matchless. Throughout many journeys, we ate well at our favorite restaurants in Bali, including Kafe Batan Waru and Siam Sally, both belonging to our generous friend Gusky Suarsana.

Finally, thanks to Tim's executive assistant Christin Markmann for corralling all the photos into a high-resolution submission and to our Rizzoli editor Sandy Gilbert, who is one of the most professional and hardworking editors in New York. And much gratitude goes to Yolanda Cuomo, Bonnie Briant, and Bobbie Richardson of Yolanda Cuomo Design, New York, who designed *Living in Paradise* so beautifully.

—Annie Kelly and Tim Street-Porter

First published in the United States of America in 2020 by
Rizzoli International Publications, Inc.
300 Park Avenue South
New York, NY 10010
www.rizzoliusa.com

Publisher: Charles Miers
Editor: Sandra Gilbert
Design: Yolanda Cuomo Design NYC
Associate Designer: Bonnie Briant
Junior Designer: Bobbie Richardson
Production Manager: Alyn Evans
Editorial Assistance: Kelli Rae Patton, Megan Conway
Managing Editor: Lynn Scrabis

Printed in China
2020 2021 2022 2023 / 10 9 8 7 6 5 4 3 2 1
ISBN: 978-0-8478-6585-7
Library of Congress Control Number: 2019953108

Visit us online:
Facebook.com/RizzoliNewYork
instagram.com/rizzolibooks
twitter.com/Rizzoli_Books
pinterest.com/rizzolibooks
youtube.com/user/RizzoliNY
issuu.com/Rizzoli

Page 1: A peaceful village lane in Sayan, Bali
Pages 2-3: A spectacular view of the Ayung River from the Taman Bebek hotel in Sayan, Bali
Pages 6-7: The stepped-down swimming pools at Bali's Amankila hotel
Pages 8-9: Travel posters from the earliest days of travel to Indonesia